EXPEDITION UNKNOWN

Beyond The Vale Publishing

Fortune Mahasha

Fortune The Hurricane

EXPEDITION UNKNOWN

Dedication

A dream is a series of thoughts, images, and sensations occurring in a person's mind during sleep and passion is strong and barely controllable emotion. All you need to achieve your goals is courage, vision and dreams plus passion also you have to hard work to whatever you believe in so that you can reach for the stars.

To My Late Father and my Late Brother

Thank you for showing love and support to me and thank you for teaching me good morals and I shall forever be grateful.

Moses Mahasha
Motswalo Ishmael Mahasha

To My Mother and my Sister

Thank you for raising me and thank you to believe in me, you taught me a value of life, peace and humanity.

Ntswake Thelma Mahasha
Eser Makatima Mahasha

To My Brothers

I can't explain how much I love you and how much it means to have you in my life.
And it's a great honour to call you my brothers.
Jones Mahasha
David Mahasha
Tiisetso Mahasha

To Kudakwashe Paul Simbi and Fortune Mupeta

Thank you for being true friends and thank you for the support and love you gave me.
Thank you for standing by me and it's a huge honour to call you my friends.

To all my teachers, lectures, friends and colleagues

Thank you so much and you will all remain a hall of fame in my books.

Contents

10

THE EXPEDITION UNKNOWN
By Fortune Mahasha, Aka Fortune the Hurricane

Over the rainbow
I have seen seven distinct colours
Above the sky,
They were chanting my name
Through thunderous sounds,
My happy was deep within myself.

The drops of rain were chanting,
Cheering and clapping for me,
I smile.
Walking out of a black shoe,
That was spotted black and white.
The wheels were spotted black and silver,
Whilst shining too.
Dancing to a rhythm,
And beat that I created.

ABUSE

By Fortune Mahasha, Aka Fortune the Hurricane

While living inside the fierce,
I woke up blue-eyed,
A river of tears on my face
No one could show me where to hide
A heartless, hungry and trousered lion
A deserted room without a coin
Molested as if it was time to graze!

I was being pushed beside the bed
And had been forced to lie on top of it.
Been forced to open my legs,
And blood was flowing between my legs,
Like a river to the sea.
I was screaming
Nobody but nobody
Could even hear me
And I could not scratch.
My soul was shackled,
My heart was untamed
And caged in an empty room
No one, but no one, came to help me.

HOPE

By Fortune Mahasha, Aka Fortune the Hurricane

I smile, the reason
Being hope,
Hope can win,
Hope can conquer,

Hope is my precious gem,
Hope can achieve,
It can fire any challenges,
Like a burner that emits and moulds a flame.

Hope can cure the broken-hearted,
Hope can heal our swollen sores,

It brings light so near,
And draws me near my dreams,
Hope can kill with its kindness,
If regaled with ingenuity.

GENDER-BASED VIOLENCE

By Fortune Mahasha, Aka Fortune the Hurricane

A cry from afar,
Begging for help,
Living in the abusive cliffs,
With heartless, cruel and hungry parasites,
Sucking blood from the veins of children and women,
Taking life from them.

Oh! No, no,
Tell me why
Do you take pride in stabbing and severing the spirit of
women and children?
Why do you hide under theology
to cover your barbarity?

Oh!
Why is this my motherland so dishevelled and sloppy?
My tears never dry,
Like the water of the oasis,
My eyes are heavy with the rain of pain and agony,
My heart is smashed like a shattered glass.

Women and children are mortal too and not critters.

HEAR MY VOICE

By Fortune Mahasha, Aka Fortune the Hurricane

I'm the first citizen of my motherland,
The child of the black soil
Africa my Africa,
Who is being refuted his citizenship,
By the self-proclaimed chief and kings.

I sit with them at the round table,
With a shrivelled tummy,
Making their biased decisions,
Without consulting the children of Africa,
Don't take my memory back to apartheid,
Where the children of Africa were being looked down
upon,
By puppets of the west and their allies.

Take me back,
Where I will be much appreciated,
Take me back,
Where I will be honoured as a devoted child of the soil.

Oh, no!
I'm tired of worshipping their idol gods,
At their satanic shrines.
I'm the tree of life,
And the seed of Africa,
Where culture and children's rights were empirical.

Give me a break,
And let me demand my rights and my tranquillity,
Without being harassed by the gun barrels.

Let me in,
And let me demand my children's participation in
politics and social welfare.

Let me in,
And have my voice in the council of the legal fraternity.

IF LOVE WAS NATURE

By Fortune Mahasha, Aka Fortune the Hurricane

If love was nature
I could have been strolling in the garden of Eden,
Singing holy harmonious songs of old-time religion,

Oh!
If love was nature,
Adam and Eve would have not savoured the forbidden
fruit,
For it was against the dogmas of God,

Nature is life,
So is love,
Love is divine,
So is nature,
Let us all feast with nature
And understand its power!

Look at the stars in the universe
They are endorsing our love,
Because it is sacred,
Let's share this moment
Concurrently in the sensations of love,

I yearn for love,
I cry for peace of heart
You came when I desired you the most, my sweet,
My soul sings for you like the grass is singing,
Come let us dance to the holy
Tune and praise the Lord!
Don't be ashamed for it is sacrosanct.

I'm addicted to you,
Like a pain killer that can heal emotional discomfort.
Let nature preach our love to the world.

If nature was love,
We could have been dwelling in a castle,
Sitting with kings and queens of the west,
Exchanging our humour!

THE WEDDING DAY

By Fortune Mahasha, Aka Fortune the Hurricane

Ooh, dear love!
I remember our wedding day,
When the clouds caressed us in approval of our union,
And the sun was not mad at us.

That day I felt a burning fire in my bones,
I placed the drops of vermilion on your forehead,
It was a divine blaze,
Sent upon us like a dove
Descending upon the son of man.

We exchanged our souls,
And we became one flesh,

We traded our vows,
You and me.

We caressed and kissed,
In front of our haters,
It was so amazing!

Remember, the diamond ring
And the nuptial necklace,
That I tied to your hand
As a symbol of our love,
It is what completes our matrimony!
I wish our betrothal will last forever,
Until it's the time to join our progenitors,
I wish to have a sunbath again,
Like the one,
we had on that day,
During the twilight!

MY VOICE

By Fortune the Hurricane and Give Heart

Dear Lord!
Why do I sound like a cub ....?
My eyes are filled with tears of sorrow.

Oh, Lord!
Over the everlasting mountain,
Where echoes are a fire, with the ability to restore my
voice!
All that I am breathing is confusion,
Due to this voice that needs attention.

Oh, Lord!
Why is this happening to me?
My spectrum is torn apart,
Enlighten my path and rekindle every part.

Oh, countless drops of bewildering
Water is raining on me,
How embarrassed I am to speak with others
Just a single word enables torturing feathers.
Almighty God,

I am ashamed to speak, but only you can enlighten me to utter without blemishes.

CHANGE THE STARS

By Fortune Mahasha, Aka Fortune the Hurricane

The stars shine beyond our imagination,
And that thrills humanity,
It let us get choked by the air of life and sired us.
Our hearts beat like a rock,
Humans are behind the images of life, not mirrors.

They departed from our own to there.
End up been departed from an elusive place with no
light, but darkness
Look across the ocean,
Look beyond the breakers,
Far out there beyond the curve
Far beyond ourselves are chainless behind the slipway.

It erupts the heart of human beings like volcano
eruption,
Painting bleaching cream out of the heartbeat,
End up choked by stars
That plug my soul to that starburst.

THE NIGHT BETRAYED MY SKIRT

By Fortune Mahasha, Aka Fortune the Hurricane

It was a night when I came home
The road of wet thorns
No one could vacate, branches blew from east to west
To the sound of the air, everyone was deaf.

The wall hit my breath
And a heavy rain surrounded me.
Two hungry lions caught my breath,
And hung at the end of the rope
Cutting my skirt into pieces.

I was like a dog wooing by the roadside,
But not even my neighbours could hear me until the
clothes reluctantly
Betrayed my body.
Lying there with nothing to cover my skin,
Blood gushing from where my legs meet.
While the lions satisfied their hunger.

My world started dimming,
Until it was like a room without a window.

Woke up in a place coloured in white,
Which smelt like a laboratory.
My eyes were greeted by a smiling elderly man,
Slowly I remembered the two lions feasting on me.
I felt tears streaming from my sore eyes.
From that moment,
My life took a turn.

Now I feel like a lepton,
Loneliness is my new bestie
Every man I see is a monster.
I feel like strangling them,
Will my life ever be like a rainbow,
Like before that night betrayed my skirt?

MY DEAR MOTHER

By Fortune Mahasha, Aka Fortune the Hurricane

Oh! My dear mother!
The true face of nature.
You have been on my side since forever,
Your beauty represents your kindness.
Filled with warmness,
You taught me how to catch a fish.
You are truly an African woman.

Oh! Dear mother!
My sunshine,
You brought joy into my life
You are truly my star,
You were by my side
When I needed you.
Thank you, my dear mother.

THE CHERISHABLE QUEEN OF AFRICA

By Fortune Mahasha, Aka Fortune the Hurricane

Africa my Africa,
Look here and there,
See the beauty of nature,
The beauty that is associated with African women.

Winnie Nomzana Madikizela Mandela,
The only queen that possesses
true characteristics of a natural queen,
The lovely rose that never withers,
It's ever-blooming like the morning sunshine.

You are the pillar of feminism,
A woman who believed in integrity, justice and women
empowerment.

The shinning stone of African beauty,
Beauty is your totem,
With your beauty, you lift the broken souls,
And make them whole again,
You gave hope to the hopeless

27

Homes to the homeless,
You will always remain an epitome of Africa,
A mother to the orphans.

You are the true force of nature
Winnie Madikizela Mandela,
Generosity is your name,
Who did not know about you?
If not the people of Soweto and beyond,

I wish to have a face-to-face conversation with you
wherever you are,

You will always remain a heroine to many in Africa,
Your name will always be remembered,
History and nature will always remember you, mama.

HEAR MY TALE

By Fortune Mahasha, Aka Fortune the Hurricane

Oh! Dear life!
I walked the solitude land,
With no one but myself,
Running away from life.
The guest that everyone is scared of entered my house,
I tried to run away,
But it was busy giggling behind me.

The night was so dark and cruel,
Nobody, but nobody in my family
Could show they are smiling stones.
Escaping the gigging sounds of death was not easy,
And it ended up taking the head of the family.

The tears were streaming,
Tearing pains and sorrows upon me.
Digging a hole without an end,
Contracting the sounds of loneliness in my heart,
My body was hanging on top of the moon
And my soul departed into the fiery air.

The shining stone on my tongue
End up departing from my mouth.
The sounds of happiness and love flew away from me,
It was all gone.

THE HEROES

By Fortune Mahasha, Aka Fortune the Hurricane

Africa, Africa, Africa!
And, your kinsmen around the continent,
Listen and listen.
First, it was a dream,
Then an idea
To a dogma that shaped the esprit of children
A philosophy that was established by Eglentyne Jebb,
To protect the youngsters.

She was fighting in the year 1919,
Protesting for children's rights,
And their position in society,
Economics and politics.

Then came the year 1923,
Rebirth of a voice!
It was born to create the sky blue
To develop a loving atmosphere,
The voice became an everlasting echo for children,
The voice that fascinated the whole continent.

She was vocalizing the song,
Singing it globally.

The sound tickles the ears and hearts of many nations.
The sea,
The ocean,
The river
And the grass was singing her personality,
Globally.
The new hero born Steve Mills,
Carries the legacy around the globe,
Born to discover,
To conquer,
To build,
To live,
To reach the summit.
The voice flowing like a river,
The Blue Roses review the true love of humanity.

The sun and the stars began to shine,
Shining for the new generation.
The storm of justice was singing,
Singing with love,
Singing with guidance.
From influential business tycoons,

Shining in the sky,
The voice flying globally.

Warming all around the lovely rose
For the truth shall remain.

A LETTER TO YOU, DEAR
By Fortune Mahasha, Aka Fortune the Hurricane

Oh, dear!
You left me with a broken heart,
My heart is smashed like the strings of a broken guitar.
All because you left for an elusive land,
It hurts so much to see you so far from me.
I know that words are like bullets in human beings, the
heart will vanish too,
But not my heart,
I hope my feelings are enough,
To explain how I miss you, dear.
My heart is bare now,
Because you left me a bachelor,
For no reason,
You left me in a location that leads to nowhere.

I hope my feelings will become everlasting love for you,
I hope to meet you at the sugarcane mountain.

Oh dear!
My heart is singing your name internally and externally,
Even if you are no more,

My heart is still singing your name,
And it never stops singing.
You have positioned me in a puzzle of love,
Where I cannot reach the hands of time.
You are the dawn and the twilight of my life,
I wish to spend the rest of my life in your absence,
Romancing with the past
Memories that we shared before,
At the sugarcane mountain.

CHILD PROTECTION

By Fortune Mahasha, Aka Fortune the Hurricane

The silence is echoing,
Rise and protect the child,
From the crocodile.

The voices of the children
Are singing power and freedom,
In revolutionary spirit.
For the hegemony to protect fresh roses,
Protecting the authorities of tomorrow against violence.

The truth can never be hushed,
When the voice of tranquillity and freedom speaks,
The tree of tomorrow is ripe and ready,
The tree of life is eager to bless and curse
The truth can never be calmed.
Trees and seas are singing in unison,
Singing a song of liberation and recognition,
In all sectors of the economy globally.

Nations and continents are not recognising the children,
They have turned a blind eye against them,

Protect the child from abuse
And all forms of unrest,
Hear the voice of the child in this pandemic epoch.
Let the roses blossom,
And allow them to shine.

THE BLEEDING HANDS

By Fortune Mahasha, Aka Fortune the Hurricane

Deeper and deeper
Into the grave,
The proud souls are crying for dew,
Turning all around the sarcophagus of consensus.
The hands of assassins bleeding blood,
Resting was not for evildoers.
Sleeping with one eye unlocked,
Their hearts are dark,
Darker than the twilight.

The white clothes standing behind them,
Looking here
And there,
Set in the pale plump faces
Wooing at them
And the horror struck once more.
Crying and tearing pains and sorrows upon them,
The horror some struck between the souls,
Shadows become their sleepless nights.
And giggling behind their ears,
Scary, and terror looms over them

Flows in a pour oil on the trouble rains,
And the pitiful faces look upon them
Turning their lives into an abyss.
And striving
But not done,
Dusty but dirty
Not knowing the deeds they did,
End up with tears of regret.

CRAZINESS OF LOVE

By Fortune Mahasha, Aka Fortune the Hurricane

When stars begin softly to spatter
Milky drops in my heart,
I will not walk away from it,
I will travel in the craziness of love,
Swim around the fairy tales
Until I meet my love by the gas works wall.
She used to possess my life like a fairy tale,
But the little lovely dream that I cried for, perished.
The love I craved for
since day one,
Has suddenly vanished.

I'm seeing and hearing the facets of love around me,
I'm not getting love
Even though I try to reach for it.
Yet, just on the paper
And messages via social media,
Oh! It was the love that I got
The love that I was in
Was not for the deepest part of the heart,
It was pointed on the papers.

Shining with its own futures,
She sits sun-dried
And sun-trapped inside me.
All those films of love; songs,
Poetry and greeting cards,
Never kissed me.
Although love is divine,
Only a few birds truly feel it.
All the rains falling on me trapped in a triangle of love lie
bleeding,
The ceiling leaks above me
And the stars around me gleam,
They made me sit in a corner
And to smile with nobody but myself.

Why does the hard dare seize the fire inside me?
Oh!
All I want is to feel the hum
And that love melody,
The love bells ring from sunrise until sunset.
For me, love is easily shaken,
All I want is that sweet rain to fall on top of my soul.
And those sweet melodies of sweet cheerful songs,
To sing for me like a love bird
Love is like a business deal.

I MISS YOU, DADDY!

By Fortune Mahasha, Aka Fortune the Hurricane

Oh! DADDY!
I yearn for the warm hands of yours,
But they are nowhere to be found.
I miss the smiles that used to cross your lips,
And the hugs that you used to give.
Now my life is trapped in the darkness,
I am a car without an engine.

Not even millions of wasps,
Could separate my mind from you.

Ever since you joined the circle of life,
My life is in shambles
The songs played during our days,
Simply ingredients perished within the blink of an eye.

Oh! Dear!
I miss the lovely rustic moments we spent,
From sunrise to sunset.
Now I'm like a tuba that's lost a tune,
The moments that we vocalized with soprano,

Gone without goodbye.
Now the grass echoes in the bushes for you,
The harmonious and melodious songs gone,
And gone forever,
To the land of the unknown.

A LETTER TO MINISTERS OF EDUCATION

By Fortune Mahasha, Aka Fortune the Hurricane

Oh! Dear Ministers!
I have a bleeding pen,
Which I placed on writing a note for you.
My heart is broken like the strings of a broken guitar,
You have offered us a place of imparting knowledge,
But it's nothing
but a place of anxiety.
You provided us with an anxiogenic,
That wipes the dreams of the innocents.
Our minds are being ruled by knowledge,
Knowledge that evicts us from our dreams.

We are in anxietude by the uninformative palace,
That vomits us into the world of the dumbstruck.
And it blinds our brains into night blindness,
Oh! Dear!
What if
We all were filled with disquietude in mentalism,
By this knowledge
That yearns for attention?

Who will lead this nation if we are all anxious,
O joo, o joo!
Save the leaders of my motherland!

TRILLIONS OF STARS

By Fortune Mahasha, Aka Fortune the Hurricane

Far beyond the sky,
And hexagrams shine within.
I can't count them,
Looking at the sky
And I can't count them
Raising sleeves higher,
But still, I can't reach
Moon mood pitches me down.

Put and paw over the moon landed,
Moon peeped through my lips.
And star crossed my lineage,
Tick had still not to gratis
And sorrel planet I stay in.

Burnt and very marvel to see,
Full and we'll round glad.
Flattered and splendid too,
And very immortal to see
Always bellows like a bull.

Hordes many times,
Still, I could not reach
But very rare
And very afar.
Deeper and deeper thicket in
And finally, ship out.

THE CHAMPION OF MY MOTHERLAND

By Fortune Mahasha, Aka Fortune the Hurricane

Oh! Dear Freddy Ramonyia,
The champion of my motherland,
Oh! South Africa, South Africa,
The land of the living dreams,
The land of the lovely rose.
That grows on the everlasting mountain,
Now listen to the shouts of jubilations
That children's president established.

Dear Freddy,
Your voice has uplifted us from an elusive land,
To the land of dreams,
And to the promising land.
Your words dismiss heavy waves around us,

You have brought the summit to my motherland,
You have become a father to the fatherless,
You have made the sky tear the tears.

You have built the voice of the wheelers,
You have turned the surface of my motherland,
The caregivers give the little roses of the living soil.
You are the lion of the living soil,
The seas and oceans sing for your name,
Internally and externally.

MAMA AFRICA

By Fortune Mahasha, Aka Fortune the Hurricane

Africa, Africa
The land of black, white
And grey soils.
The land that contracts the beauty of nature,
You are the black rock of Africa,
You are the tree of life.
Nobody can define your strength,
You have raised your children with love
And nobody matches your kindness.
You are the mother of all nations,
The supreme rock of Africa
You are queen of queens.
Your beauty represents the beauty of an African queen,

Common lands can't compete with you,
Your land is free from farming,
Mining,
Fishing,
And hunting.
A continent that's incomparable,
The nation that's strong in the spirit of humanity.

From northern and eastern,
From western to southern Africa.

You have planted seeds of tropical roses,
The agricultural land is our pattern.
Travelling zone of diamonds,
Coal,
And gold.
We are there,
The oceans, seas
And rivers sing our personalities.
Agricultural patterns are our life,
Rainy seasons are our treasures.
The root of value is our middle name,
Africa, Africa is the land of the iron thorns.

JUNE

By Fortune Mahasha, Aka Fortune the Hurricane

The time of the youth,
The gathering together with the youth comrades,
Vindicating the voicelessness of the youthhood.
Celebrating the voice given to us,
By the youth comrades of 19th
The youth of tomorrow,
You are the youth comrades of today and tomorrow,
When we remember our youth comrades of the 20th
century,
The spirit of the comrades is shattered like the strings of
a broken guitar.

We are walking on the land that's undeveloped,
The land of the youth comrades.
No one wants to hear us,
No, no, no
Take me back to that time,
Where the youth comrades were appreciated,
And heeded to.
We are the innocents comrades,

That walk on the fuelled streets.

Let us strive,
For humanity of all youth comrades.
Let us unite,
And build Africa
And our home of peace.
Let us build Africa, our land.

BORN IN JULY

By Fortune Mahasha, Aka Fortune the Hurricane

Oh! Heavenly lord
The day I was born,
The sky was blue
And with cold air inside the yard.
Pebbles of water pounding on the head,
Flowing like rain on my head.

Outside was windy,
The surface of the day was cold
And warm at the same time.
The trees were od from summer,

The sky was crying,
And taking out the tears from the cattle,
The shadow flag raised the wasp on the body.
The bush was wet
And I could not penetrate it,
It was dusty,
And I could not see it
The bushes were blowing from west to east point.
The earth couldn't accept my silent ghost body,

THE BRIGHT LIGHT

By Fortune Mahasha, Aka Fortune the Hurricane

Oh! Dear bright light,
Pass through my eyes,
To remove the silent ghost inside me.
Darkness couldn't vacate my house,
Where water is thirsty to hunt for my soul.

Its chain locked my chest,
And I couldn't run.
The stream is running,
And surrounded me.
It bites like a wasp in the night,

Running like a runaway train,
Dusty the anagrams inside my hands,
The bright light clop, clop
And clop.
And I couldn't see it or carry it.

It winked bright like a diamond,
And I couldn't wink for the sunshine.
It winked,
But the darkness couldn't penetrate the light.

DUSTY LAND

By Fortune Mahasha, Aka Fortune the Hurricane

There was dust back at home,
No one could hide from the wind dust.
It blows into four points,
And nobody could carry it.
It soaked us
And buried us above the crust,
The dusty road was not a promontory place to land,

The dust stream, that winter dust,
Crossed the burglar-proofing of the house.
And skeltered through the place,
No one could carry it.

The trees and houses were shackled, caged,
The seed could hear our footsteps,
No one could cross it.
It silenced the cries,
And the wasp bit us like a vampire.
Nobody but nobody could escape the dust stream.

THE DARK TEEN NIGHT

By Fortune Mahasha, Aka Fortune the Hurricane

The teen night,
Deep into the deepest of the night
Thicker in the dark night.
Teens turn thirsty,
The souls are bleeding through the brain.

The head buries the hatchet,
Dust flatters our faces to be pale.
The darkness carves us limb to limb,
Tears loom upon us.
Dust shadows our shadows,
And no one could stop it.

The anger bone blocks the chest,
And we could not chugg after bugger;
It plagues on its mouth.

TRUST BEYOND THE MINDSET

By Fortune Mahasha, Aka Fortune the Hurricane

Trust clocking
And clocking over the mindset,
It rusts the live-thing
And no one can hold it.
The sounds thrills the mind over the edge point,

Trust it flag ecstatic shallows over us,
Swing upside and down.
It evicts shadows and erupts from the true,

Clopping up and down,
And rust the mind off
It turns into dust,
And vanish forever.

THE DIRECTION OF LIFE

By Fortune Mahasha, Aka Fortune the Hurricane

How far time is,
No one wants to hold it.
It flies all around the spheres,
But nobody can click it.
Earthen around the weave
Clock and nobody but nobody can wear around it,

It is the diviner of human beings,
And everything changes within the eye of the clock,
Just like winter gives way to spring
And darkness gives way to brightness.

Oh!
How life can be so unfair,
It creates a maze of troubles for us,
Across the moon trapped our trousers.
And four cardinal points road turn us pale,
No one could vacate its way.

Oh!
Nobody, but nobody could see it,

Pounding rain of tears upon us,
And it flows like a river.

TRAGIC LIFE

By Fortune Mahasha, Aka Fortune the Hurricane

Not only how far life may go,
But tears will never vacate our heartbeat,
It comes out of the enemy city
Where it couldn't link the way out.
It winged out the happiness within,
It clocks the breath out of the lungs,
Tautly strung like antennae.

It backhand slaps the vulnerable
And I could not see it,
It springs off the mood.
Nervous and irritating too,
It blocked the chest until death
And sired us to the forbidden land,

The sound crushed us down to existence,
It robbed us of our joy.
The air choked us,
And bit our souls.

TRAGIC SONGS OF THE CITY OF GOLD

By Fortune Mahasha, Aka Fortune the Hurricane

I was standing there in the solitude,
Awoken with the sunset.
Gaze at my beloved once of Johannesburg,
Turning into wasps beyond the evil mountains.
Before the sunrise gunshots
Cross my doorstep,
Passing through the maddening night.
And hammering the earth surface of Johannesburg,

Flying west and to east,
And bites the soul.
And blood waves through the sea,
Waving around the innocents
The sons appear stiff with weapons.
That are shackled,

Elder drinks sold like juice for kids,
And smack the brains of our generation.
Its bite is morefold,
And itches in the hearts of the immortal.

CHANGES OF LIFE

By Fortune Mahasha, Aka Fortune the Hurricane

Oh! Dear Lord,
This life changes like a wheel changing the earth
direction,
It's so ruthless sometimes,
And it backhand slaps the vulnerable.
It thrills the ears of human beings,
And it bites the brain with anxiety.

It alters the circle of life like a tree,
The valleys drain the darkness to us,
And climate it does vanish.
It travels around the wheels
And bites toes like hungry rats,
Makes us fogbound to the solitudes.
And leaves us lonely and forgotten.

MIGRANT CHILDREN

By Fortune Mahasha, Aka Fortune the Hurricane

I'm the solitaire child in my own motherland,
Migratory bird without hope.
Watching my beloved people of Africa being separated,
Separated from one place which is called home.
Waving my hand through a maze of troubles,
That lay with me at night.
The streets were cold and treated me evilly,

Oh! Dear,
It's so heartless to watch my siblings hide under a cold
spring,
The species of my world were murdered.
Cold death loomed over,
Like an angry wasp.
And wiped my loved ones far beyond,
Our faces in the mirror stare accusingly at us.
Thinking how to leave another chapter.
And pin us to wear long faces.
Flee from a stream,
And maddening in the chest.

It robs us of our home,
And leaves us homeless.
Oh! How I wish the truth has a tongue,
To vomit the reality,
And set us free from the stream.

THE MOTHER OF NATURE

By Fortune Mahasha, Aka Fortune the Hurricane

The sound of the bushes,
Interestedly reviews the strength of nature.
The colours of morate the everlasting mountains,
And show your kindness.
The beauty of your eyes sip the words out
Of our mouth,

The images of love, life and joy.
Reboot the love of humanity,
And your songs plant peace within.
The fairies wait for your gifts,
It brings humanity and unity to us,
And open the stars in the sky.
The roses uplift the spirit of nature
And the air shows the freedom of our land,
Freedom of humanity,
Freedom of nature.
Freedom of expression,
And your beauty will never be resilient.

MY HERO, NELSON MANDELA

By Fortune Mahasha, Aka Fortune the Hurricane

South Africa, South Africa,
The land of my first president,
The country of peace.
Where ancient rivers
Flow to the eyes of the beholders.
When he was breaking rocks
They thought they were breaking his spirit.
Not at all,
When the battalions of the white fleas,
Dusted the land of living dreams,
And he uttered No, not with my people,
He penetrated the wet bushes, maddened by fleas.

My first black president,
You were our political father
And a father to the fatherless.
Freedom and hero of men
And women, you became our gospel,
When dust was dusting our nation,
You fought like a warrior.
Your motherland praised your name,

You warmed our nation's eyes.
And brought back the summit,

Your word became our sunshine in our heads,
Your voice uplifted the black voice and a white voice,
You became a contract for our freedom.
You will forever remain a hero Ntate Nelson Mandela,
Who does not know about you?
What if?
If not politicians, women and men of your liberating
politics work,
Free us from the shambles of this world!
I wish to meet you in the everlasting mountains.

THE OLD MORNING JOY OF THE WEST

By Fortune Mahasha, Aka Fortune the Hurricane

The wind slips from east to west,
Below the rose tree.
The seed rotates around the edge of the heart.
The heart is tearing, the palms sweat.
And powering the bubbling heart,

Shining the lovely rose out of the vacuole,
Shooting the lonely heart with love and kindness.
Not going to stop it,
Bilking the sweet smile out of the mouth.

Dancing below par on the white suet of the sky,
Digging on the rooftop of the heart.
Spring love on top of it,
And the beauty shuts the pale plump face.

THE LONELY NIGHT
By Fortune Mahasha, Aka Fortune the Hurricane

The night in the dark,
Travelling to the east.
With no one on the road but myself,
The battalions of wasps were gathered beside the road,
And nobody could vacate the evil road alone,
Nobody but nobody,
Could defeat the thirsty monster.

The dark clothes across the board of my eyes,
My mind was caged,
And I thought of nothing to ease myself.
My face was tearing the tears of the raindrops,
But I was silent with no sound.
My tears were breaking the echoes of silence
And I could not nothing
because I was afraid.

A GLOOMY TRAVEL IN THE DARK NIGHT

By Fortune the Hurricane and Give Heart

In the dark night,
Fierce lighting tearing the sky as if it will split.
Alone, all alone with no one on the road to soothe
The windy bushes blowing from north to south...

Hallucinations triggering the dark myths,
Rescue me Lord from this sad road.
The water is not thirsty but hungry
Came to my house talking all night long,
With no one else but me, all alone.

Wide-open become the windows,
The air blew all over me as I heard
Conversations in the condos,
Unknown to me from the invisible shadows
The scent of sadness invading my household.
With empty hopes,
I was alone.

Dripped with tears like a window wailing with dew
With pains and sorrows hovering around me like a
deserted widow,
All alone and without anybody in the hollow night.

THE MIRROR OF LIFE

By Fortune Mahasha, Aka Fortune the Hurricane

Mirror is the only divine set of our images,
And that measures our lifestyle.
It rotates around us day and night,
And can't see the madness of it.
Disenchanted to choked by the images,
Of mirrors in our own miscreants.
Which is the only diviner of human beings,

Nobody could order the phoenix of magic mirrors,
And return us to anxiety.
Angry fleas bite the heartbeat
And accuse our lives,
And remind us of the past.

Acumen mirrors intuition latent;
And snag, not bruise one heart
Mirrors, mirrors curse us to loneliness.
Life swim or sneak,
And the eyes glimpse air bud opposes the bull.

WHO WILL CROSS THE BORDER OF LIFE

By Fortune Mahasha, Aka Fortune the Hurricane

Look!
Look, side by side,
Out there,
Beyond the breakers.
With untaken roads and unclean borders,
That departed life into ashes over the mountains.
Where echoes are fired beyond the cross of life,
The harmoniousness between life and death.
The spectrum is torn apart to death,
That erupts out of the curve.

Then look across the ocean,
It departed from the sky into the hereafter.
And erupt tears in the households with rust,
And slips away from us.
Look! Look,
Far beyond the border,
Pin us to that place.

Reaching out to the sea,
Far and close the curve.
Meeting with earth and oceans,
It tore the ocean like a moon night.
It crosses the mouldboard within,

CORONAVIRUS

By Fortune Mahasha, Aka Fortune the Hurricane

Oh! Dear covid,
A bulldozer to human heat
You travel to the solitude land.
And tore my beloved ones apart,
Making countless giants fall.
And walking with an unprocurable virus around our
tenement body
That gives us nothing but flu.
It leads us to an elusive journey of life,
That contracts from a fist to a revolver.

It bit, hit the chest like a runaway train,
It vanished within our bodies.
It disrupted the organs within
And made an unpleasant illness,
Sprang the organs with dizziness.

It cut the soul into pieces
And buried the breath.

The wave of disease burst from the body like a volcanic
eruption,
It grew deeper and deeper
And shackled the souls of human beings.
It caged the body inside an empty room,

It itched the veins,
Like anger fleas.
Its pain grew deeper and deeper,
And more unpleasant within.

DEAR DARLING

By Fortune Mahasha, Aka Fortune the Hurricane

Oh! Dear darling,
Ever since I landed my eyes on you,
My heart beats faster and slower.
My palms smile within me,
I have not stopped yet,
You brought me smiles.
And gave me a rhythmic reason to live,

My heart is wearing a red jacket
That I could not take it off.
You turned darkness into brightness,
You made my heart sweet.
You are gorgeous and totally amazing too,
You are my precious treasure.
I wish time would stand still,
And it cannot, bitter pill.
Drums play in my heart like fire,
I wanted to shelter you from pouring rain.

You have warmed my heart,
And gave me a lovely rose that blooms within my heart.

MURDERED SLEEPING

By Fortune Mahasha, Aka Fortune the Hurricane

The evil eye crossed my eyes within a night,
The drops of sky bleed within.
And silent to death,
The blood was watery mucus into my lips.

The clouds' eyes were crying,
And they toasted my pale face.
It was sitting on my chest,
And I could not breathe.
The evil-minded was hammering my chest,
And feasted on my soul.

I was lying down, thinking
How to silent my ghost within me.
Evil and cruel lions sip my blood away,
The storm clouds were gathered in my own maze of
troubles,
And left me running weakly until death.

ECHOES OF ENDLESS DROPS

By Fortune the Hurricane and Give Heart

Pause the pretending smiles,
Unleash the unheard but true bells.
Soon these little ones will commence the march for
peace,
High-quality justice for these is in vain,
They need true kisses.

They are thirsty,
But this ordinary water you have can't quench it,
Hey you, office bosses,
Are you not hearing the extremely repeating sound so
bereft?
Everything has its time for happening,
Maybe you have become too hostile that you don't even
feel the saddening.

First of all, you were once small,
Rates of wailing rose like this in every mole,
Out of every corner,
Please be humane and listen to the call;
Nine hundred,

And ninety-nine million of these,
Without adequate privileges.
Terribly represented by one infrastructure of you as you
call their grievances,
"noise" as they are wailing.

Not any of these deserve a life of strife,
Old rules are still in place,
And they cannot change for your handkerchief,
Worn out are your thoughts,
Renew them for the pleasure of the everlasting chief.

TROUBLE IN PARADISE

By Fortune Mahasha, Aka Fortune the Hurricane

Oh, Oh! No, no!
What is bigger than a cricket;
Has entered a cricket hole.
It was as if I was dreaming,
It was a nightmare playing with my thoughts,
That chased me towards doom and death.
Maybe doom is my destiny,
So I must just surrender to it.

I couldn't do anything,
But to run,
It drew a pattern
And puzzle of pain and sorrows for my soul,
And doom was my middle name to wear.

MY LAST WISH

By Fortune Mahasha, Aka Fortune the Hurricane

I feel like yesterday,
Because of dance then burst,
I wish to shift my feet against the floor again,
Shift it at the sugar candy palace.

To make my breath slip out to the sky,
And let my soul come to peace within.
That is all I wish,
To see the moon
And meet before the sunset hide.

WHO AM I?

By Fortune Mahasha, Aka Fortune the Hurricane

Oh, Oh!
I'm a lion that strikes with a ghost,
I'm a lion that lay its life.
I'm a cat of my motherland,
That dwells on its pride.
I spotted white on my label,
I fight for peace
And for the spirit of the jungle.

CURSED

By Fortune Mahasha, Aka Fortune the Hurricane

Ever, since my eye crossed your face,
I dwell in sleepless nights,
My thoughts only yearn for you.
When I'm close to you,
Words vanish from my mouth.
Your beauty makes my heart overflow like a volcanic
eruption,
Your tears shine within.

Why do I feel this way?
Tell me why?
Why is your beauty so fearful to me?
Tell me why?

DAYS ARE COMING
By Fortune Mahasha, Aka Fortune the Hurricane

Oh! Dear,
Look at me,
Here I am.
I'm trouble to the waters of the mind,
Conquering the circle of hatred of my life.
The fiends with evil minds alarmed by my goal,
And approach the skysails.
Dwelling within the kings and queens of the west,
And my enemies will be wearing long faces.

GIRLFRIEND

By Fortune Mahasha, Aka Fortune the Hurricane

Oh! Dear,
I have crossed seven seas just to find you,
I know,
That we are just flatterers.
That itch our heart defends,
My feelings accuse my flaws,
And break into plural faults,
That amend and ascend within me.

THE ROAD OF TRAGEDY

By Fortune Mahasha, Aka Fortune the Hurricane

Oh!
Why did I bend and blend on this road?
Why?
Darkness tends and trends upon me,
Red road within my veins
Like drops of a vital liquid within me.
Bleeding and trending to death,
That sends and spends my existence.
My legs torn apart,
And my breath joins the shambles of my forefathers.

THE DESTROYER OF YOUTH

By Fortune Mahasha, Aka Fortune the Hurricane

OH! My motherland,
I shambled in it,
To bend down on my land.
You came to my compound,
And spent anxiety within my land
You blended our nation with your evil-minded,
You take pride in evicting our knowledge to nothing.
I can call you names,
Because you are not ashamed of your deeds.
Who sent you to spoil this world with your sickness,
Why are you so ruthless and heartless?
Tell me!
What is your real name?

THE TABULA RASA

By Fortune Mahasha, Aka Fortune the Hurricane

Deeper and deeper into the unknown,
Blends blank sheets in my thoughts
And nervous pause within,
The clean slate of my empty thoughts,
And flashes me to the unknown foe.

MEIN KAMPF (MY STRUGGLE)

By Fortune Mahasha, Aka Fortune the Hurricane

Dear!
Mr poverty-stricken,
Hear my innocent voice,
I used to wear colourless and muddy clothes,
Ranking on the street with nobody but myself.
And crying dew,
The clothes I used to wear had nothing
But gashes,
And the flies would make their way through them.

The clothes I used to wear would only cover one hung of
my flesh,
Which was the hip.
And cover me lazily,
I wept reddish tears in the night,
And swept the salty tears in the belly of the night
All because of my lifestyle.

Grumbling and rumbling loomed upon my tummy,
Slowly evicted me,
And left me growly and crankily.

BULLYING

By Fortune Mahasha, Aka Fortune the Hurricane

Tick tock,
In the belly of the wicked plural.
Crying for my soul,
Sucking blood from my veins
And tearing my soul apart.

The eyebrows torn against me,
And the sinister fisted on me;
Kept my soul in the crypt.
And left me drowning,
My tears dropping down like rain
And crying excessively.

My soul in peril,
Linking down, seeking aid,
Gone and lost in the fish's belly.
Leaving me restless,
And turning pale within an eye.

THE LEGEND WITHIN

By Fortune Mahasha, Aka Fortune the Hurricane

Tick tock,
In the time of the legends.
Dear!
Mr Mahlatse Mailula
The undefeated Strauss of Africa,
Your words of wisdom valorise the valley.
And you are the pillar of feminism.
Generosity is your name,

You are the epitome of children,
A voice to the voiceless.
A man who believes in integrity,
justice and children empowerment.
Your battles lead us to be victorious
And to the promising land
Of peace and unity,
leads us to the land of honey.

FALSE ACCUSATIONS

By Fortune Mahasha, Aka Fortune the Hurricane

Lonely in the deepest maze of confusion,
I tied my soul in the darkness.
Played a game of friendship with an evildoer,
And I was blinded by affection in her
Before,
I gave her a name, sweet cassava.
De die in diem I can't stop thinking about her.
And love bells could not stop ringing,
When my eyes landed on her,
My heart was halting in her present,
Her beauty was like the beauty of an angel.

She rejected my heart,
And my friendly requests twice,
The melody of friendship shared
Turned into a nightmare.
Her evil eyes were hidden under her skin colour,
The evil-minded under the skin of a sheep.
Greedy started loving the packet of my currency.
Slowly and slowly drove me,
Into a land of doom and destruction.

And accused me of rape,
Painted my soul with fake accusations.
All because I was filled with love for her soul,
Slowly my soul set sail towards the seven seas of doom.
To where my eyes were blinded from the sea of light,
And society rejected me.
My soul started crying for,
Behind bars.

About the author

Lehlogonolo Fortune Mahasha was born in the year 2002 in a family of six children and he is the last child. He grew up in the beautiful city of Polokwane in Mankweng and he started writing short stories in primary school before progressing to poetry in high school.

He is currently studying chemical engineering at pentagon College next to the University of Limpopo, and he is a participant at Save The Children South Africa as a child rights defender also writing articles about the issues that affect children.